thanks mum

thanks mum

inspiring thoughts for mothers

edited by tom burns

Published in the United Kingdom in 2010
by Tangent Publications
an imprint of
Axis Publishing Limited
8c Accommodation Road
London NW11 8ED
www.axispublishing.co.uk

Creative Director: Siân Keogh
Managing Editor: Brian Burns
Production Manager: Jo Ryan

ISBN 978-0-9543620-9-6

2 4 6 8 10 9 7 5 3 1

Printed and bound in China

about this book

Thanks Mum brings together an inspirational selection of powerful and life-affirming phrases about mothers and motherhood and combines them with evocative and gently amusing animal photographs that bring out the full humour and pathos of the human condition.

We all lead busy lives and sometimes forget to tell our mums how much we love them and how grateful we are for everything they do for us. These inspiring examples of wit and wisdom, written by real people based on their true-life experiences, sum up the essence of motherhood and why our mothers will always be so special to us. As one of the entries so aptly puts it – mothers make the world go around.

So give thanks to your mum and tell her you love her!

about the author

Tom Burns is a writer and editor who has written for a wide range of magazines and edited more than one hundred books on subjects as diverse as games and sports, cinema, history and health and fitness. From the hundreds of contributions that were sent to him, he has selected the ones that best sum up what being a mum is all about – giving support, encouragement and most of all, love.

A mother's love
is like a circle.
It has no beginning
and no ending.

A mother's love is forever;
time, distance, hardship...
all fall before the
strength of her love.

You never realise how much your mother loves you till you explore the attic – and find every letter you ever sent her, every finger painting, clay pot, bead necklace, Easter chicken, cardboard Santa Claus, paperlace Mother's Day card and school report since day one.

There is no friendship, no love like that of the mother for her child.

No language could express the power and beauty and heroism of a mother's love.

A mother is a blend of strength and survivorship, experience and insight, fancy and reflection.

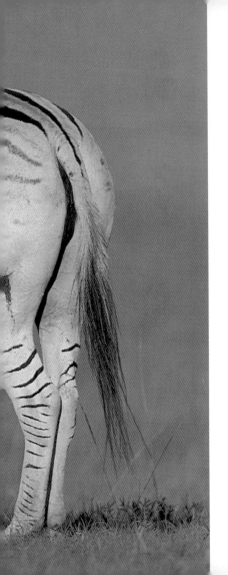

A mother is not a
person to lean on,
but a person to
make leaning
unnecessary.

You're never too
heavy for your
mother to bear.

The best mothers are
those who listen and
always understand.

A mother
understands
what a child
does not say.

A mother laughs our
laughter, sheds our tears,
returns our love and
fears our fears.

Mother is the one to whom you hurry when you are troubled.

My mum is the best –
she's a friend when I need one,
a nurse when I need one
and she's always there.

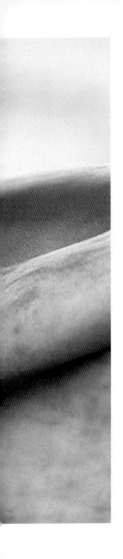

A mother is like an island
in life's ocean, a peaceful
quiet shelter from the
restless tide.

Nobody knows how to pamper like a mum.

Mother's arms are made up of tenderness and sweet sleep blesses the child who lies therein.

A mother's love
perceives no
impossibilities.

Mother love is the fuel that enables a normal human being to do the impossible.

Like kites without strings, mothers teach you to soar with your dreams.

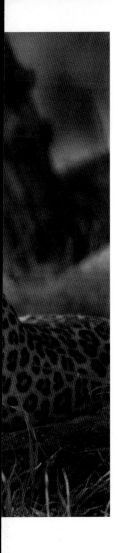

A mother's love is so strong and unyielding that it endures all circumstances: good fortune and misfortune, prosperity and privation, honour and disgrace.

A mother is a person who seeing there are only four pieces of pie for five people, promptly announces she never did care for pie.

The way to your mother's heart,
is to eat her food with relish.
(Or anything else that
disguises the taste.)

The heart of a
mother is a deep
abyss at the
bottom of which
you will always find
forgiveness.

A mother loves her children even when they least deserve to be loved.

A mother's love is not blind; it's just very nearsighted.

It's not easy being a mother.
If it were easy, fathers
would do it.

A man's work is from sun to sun, but a mother's work is never done.

A mother always has
to think twice:
once for herself
and once for her child.

Life is nothing but
a series of crosses
for mothers.

The joys of motherhood are never fully experienced until the children are in bed.

If evolution really works,
how come mothers only have
one pair of hands?

Any mother could perform the jobs of several air traffic controllers with ease.

By and large, mothers and housewives are the only workers who do not have regular time off.

Being a full-time mother is one of the highest-salaried jobs, since the payment is pure love.

A mother who is really a mother is never free.

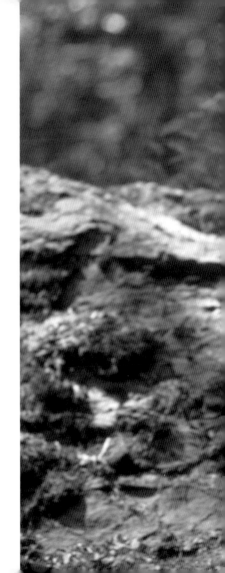

A mother holds her children's hands for a while, their hearts forever.

A man loves his sweetheart the most, his wife the best, but his mother the longest.

Youth fades, love droops, the
leaves of friendship fall;
a mother's secret hope
outlives them all.

Children and mothers never truly part – they are bound in the beating of each other's heart.

The mother's heart is the child's schoolroom.

Real mothers know that
a child's growth is not
measured by height
or years or grades.

It is marked by the
progression of Mama
to Mummy to Mother.

Men are what their mothers made them.

No matter how old a mother is, she watches her middle-aged children for signs of improvement.

Mothers are like
fine collectibles –
as the years go by,
they increase
in value.

Mothers are the only goddesses in whom the whole world believes.

Mother is the name
for God on the lips
and in the hearts
of little children.

A mother is the one through whom God whispers love to his little children.

Motherhood is a wonderful thing – what a pity to waste it on children.

Of all the rights of women,
the greatest is to be a mother.

Simply having children does not make mothers.

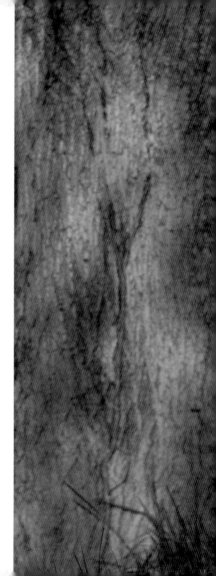

Mothers have as powerful an influence over the welfare of future generations as all other forces combined.

Mothers make the family
go around.

Mothers make
the world go around.

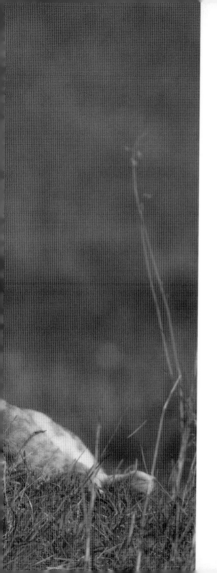

Take the word 'family.' Strike out the 'm' for mother and the 'y' for youth – and all you have left is 'fail.'

It takes a hundred
men to make an
encampment,
but one mum
to make a home.

Mother is the heartbeat
in the home.

A mother is she who can take the place of all others but whose place no one else can take.

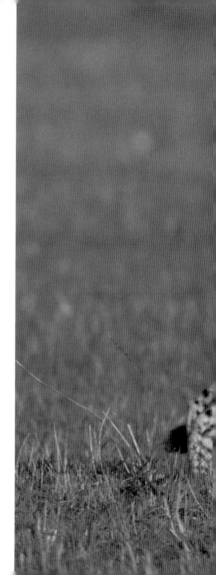

A mother is a person who if she is not there when you get home from school you wouldn't know how to get your dinner and you wouldn't feel like eating it anyway.

Of all the things that come in numbers – plenty of rainbows, stars in the sky, brothers, sisters, aunts, uncles, cousins – you have but one mother.

We only have one mum, one mummy, one mother in this world, one life. So give thanks and tell her you love her.

I'll always love you, Mum.